Three-Octave Scales

for the Cello

Book One: The Basics

by Cassia Harvey

Contents

CHP152
ISBN 978-1-932823-51-6

www.charveypublications.com

1. C major

Cassia Harvey

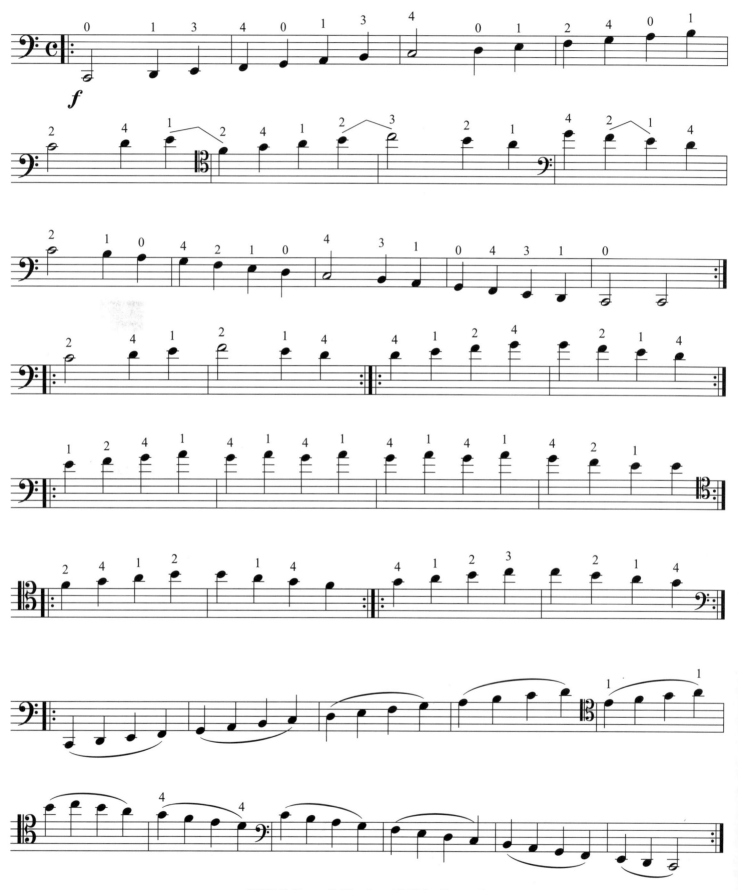

2. G major

3. D major

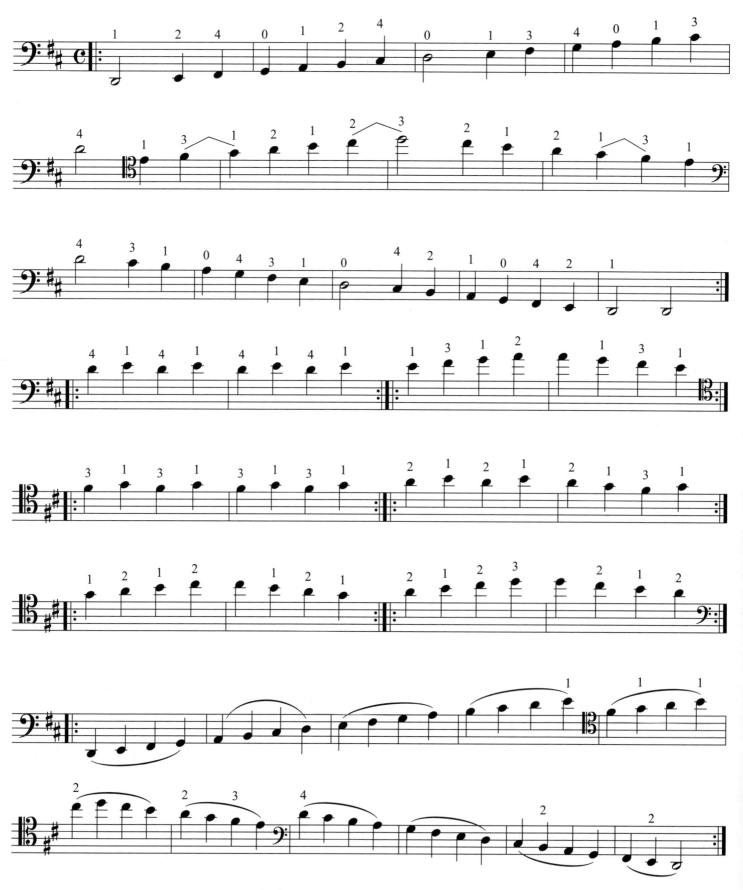

4. A major

5. E major

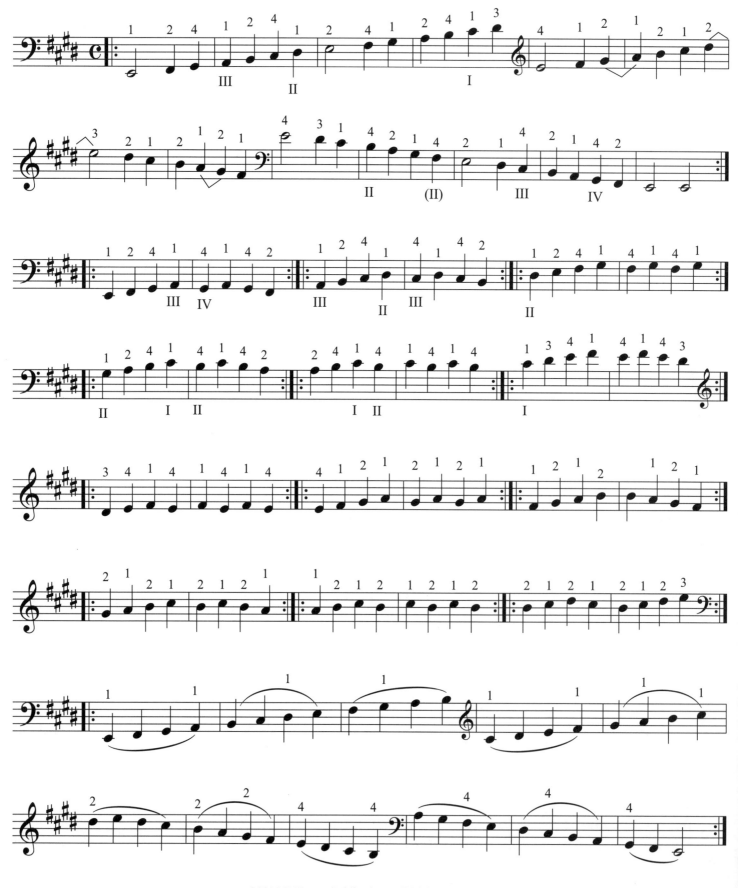

6. B major

7. F♯ major

8. D♭ major

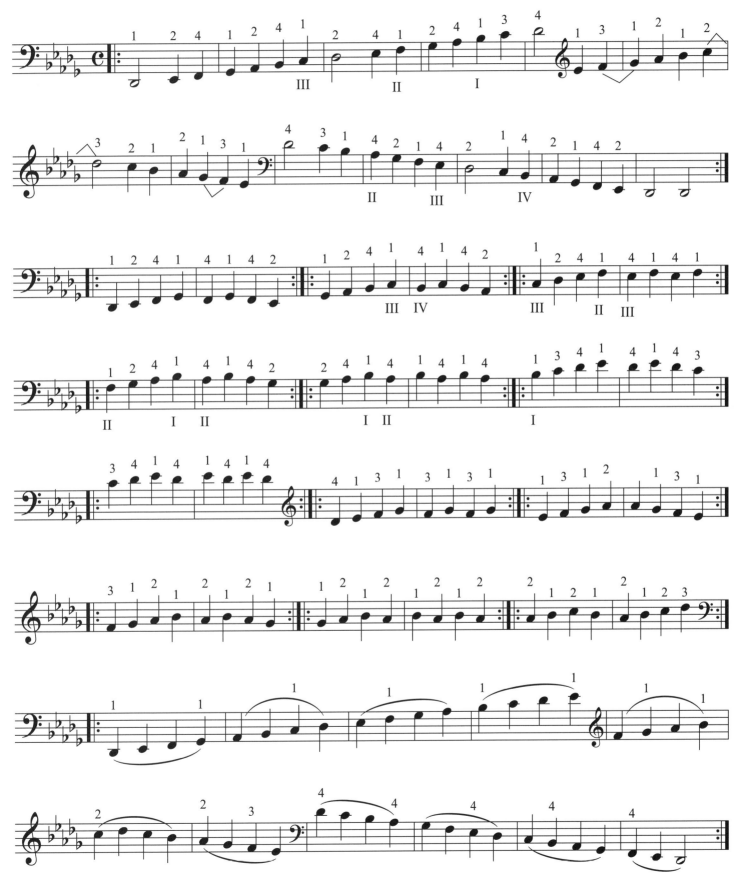

9. A♭ major

10. E♭ major

11. B♭ major

12. F major

13. A minor

Melodic

Harmonic

14. E minor

Melodic

Harmonic

15. B minor

Melodic

Harmonic

16. F♯ minor

Melodic

Harmonic

17. C♯ minor

Melodic

Harmonic

18. G# minor

Melodic

Harmonic

19. E♭ minor

Melodic

Harmonic

20. B♭ minor

Melodic

Harmonic

21. F minor

Melodic

Harmonic

22. C minor

Melodic

Harmonic

23. G minor

Melodic

Harmonic

24. D minor

Melodic

Harmonic

25. Chromatic

26. Chromatic, Slurred

27. C major

28. G major

29. D major

30. A major

31. E major

32. B major

33. F♯ major

34. D♭ major

35. A♭ major

36. E♭ major

37. B♭ major

38. F major

39. A melodic minor

40. E melodic minor

41. B melodic minor

42. F♯ melodic minor

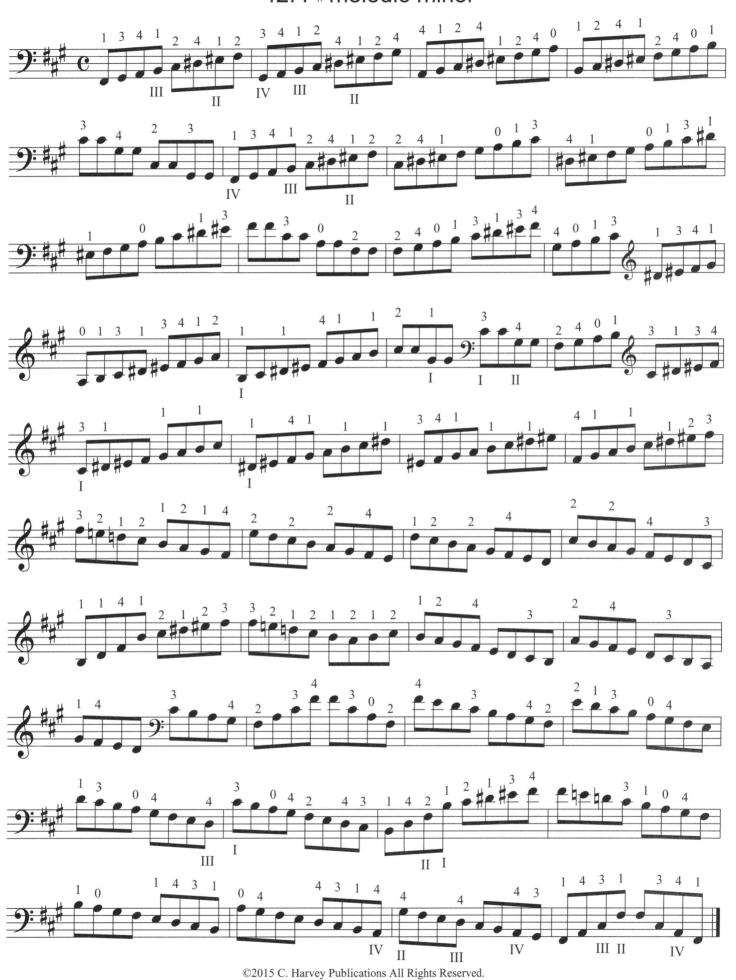

43. C♯ melodic minor

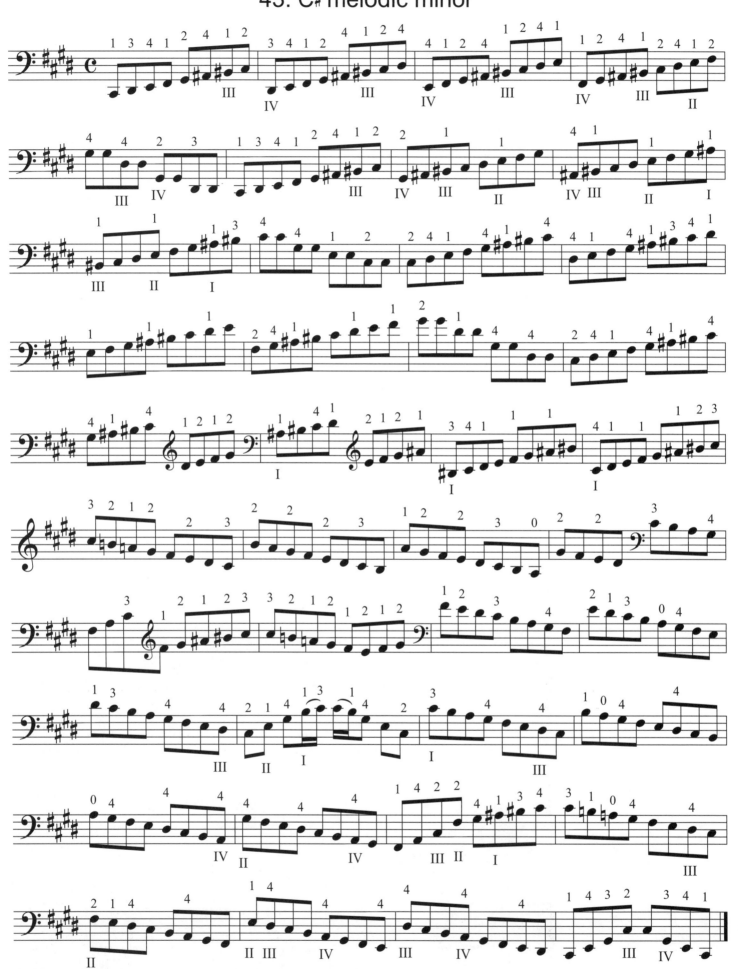

44. G♯ melodic minor

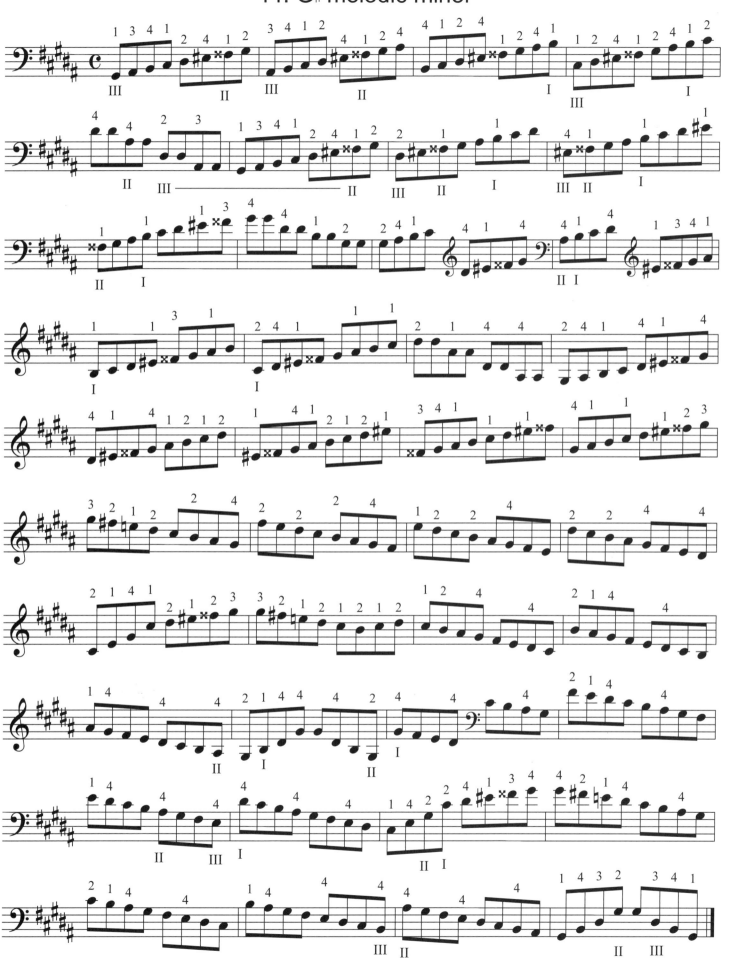

45. E♭ melodic minor

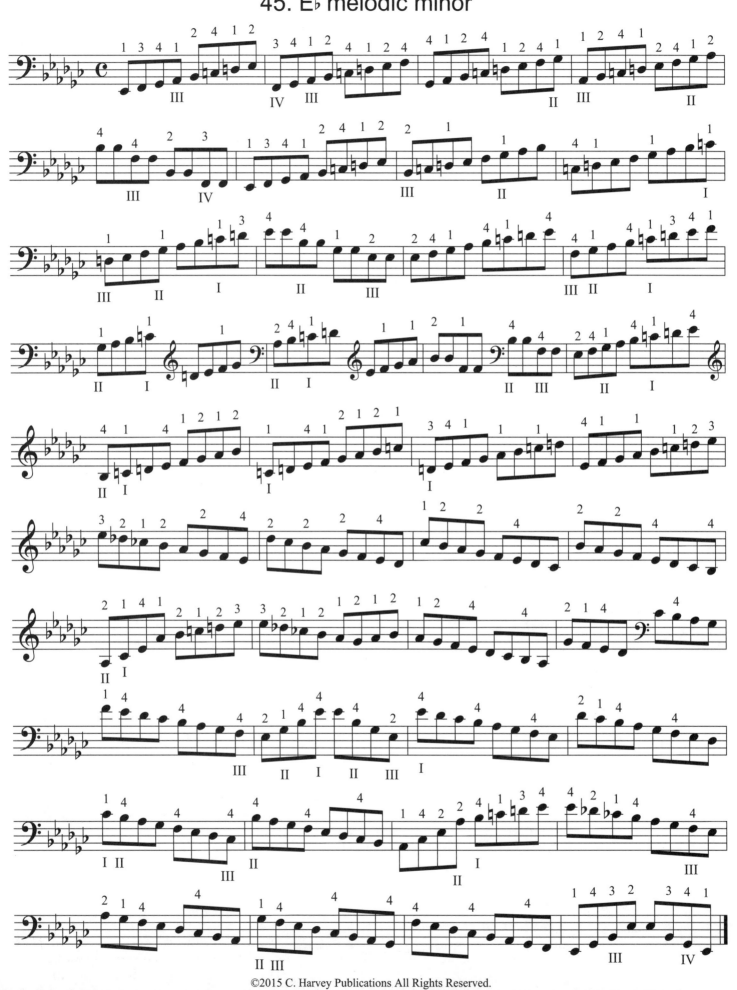

46. B♭ melodic minor

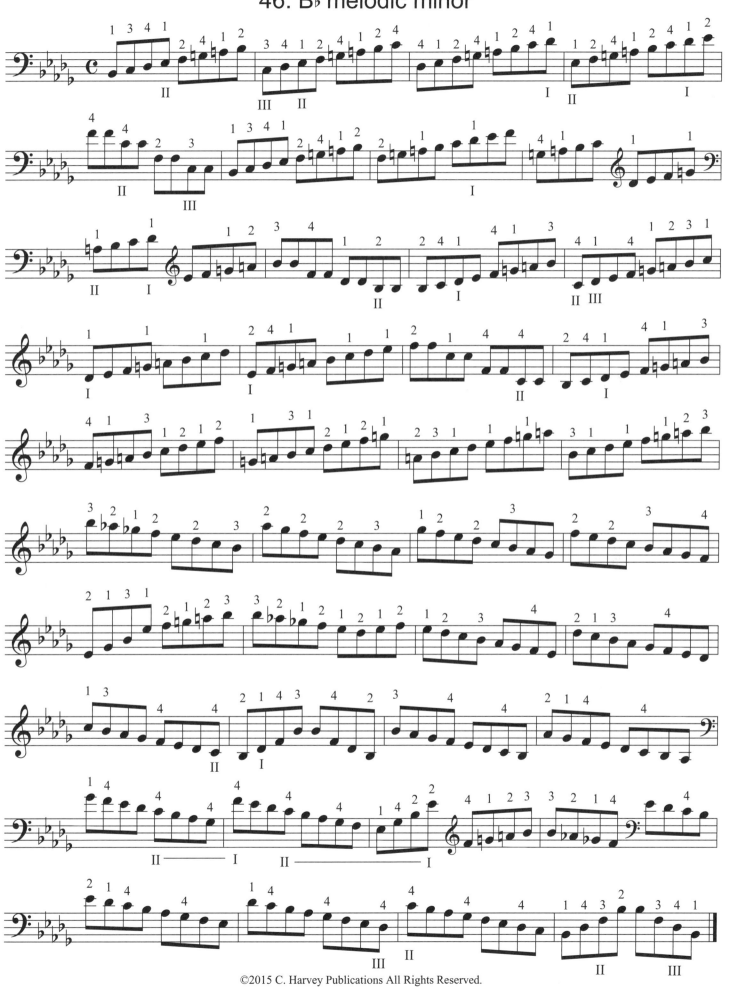

47. F melodic minor

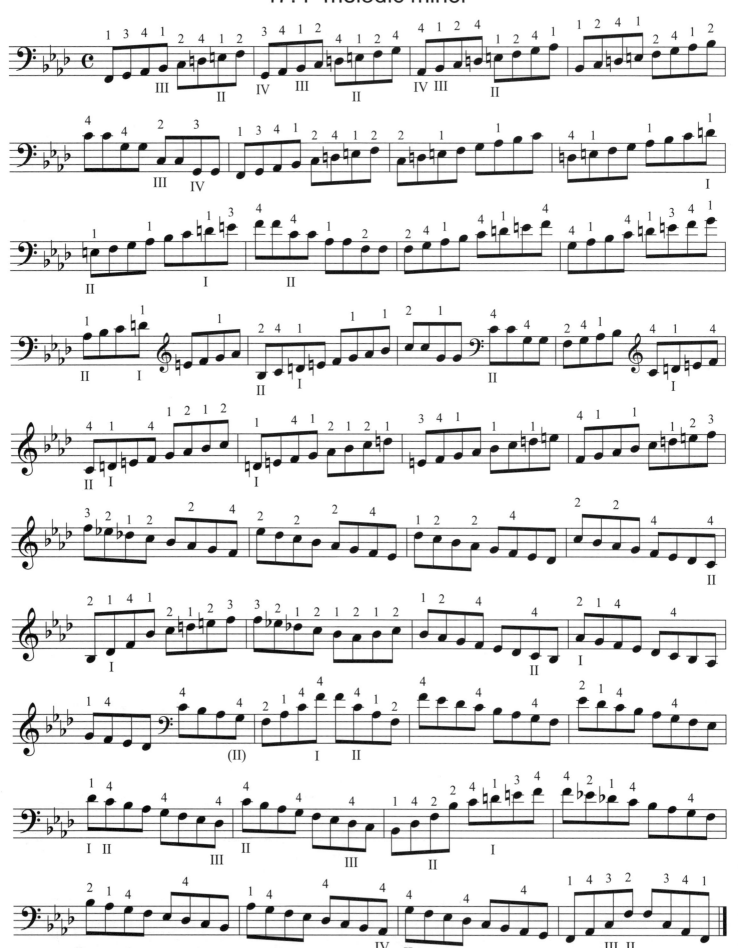

48. C melodic minor

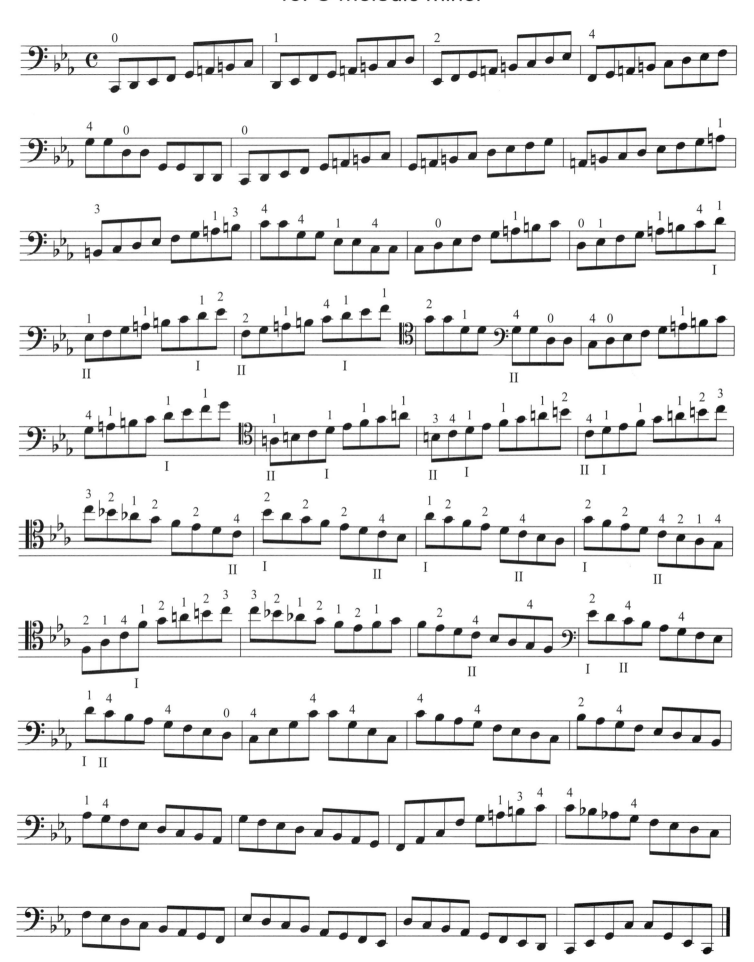

49. G melodic minor

50. D melodic minor

Three-Octave Scales for Cello, Book Two: Variations

Cassia Harvey

C Major

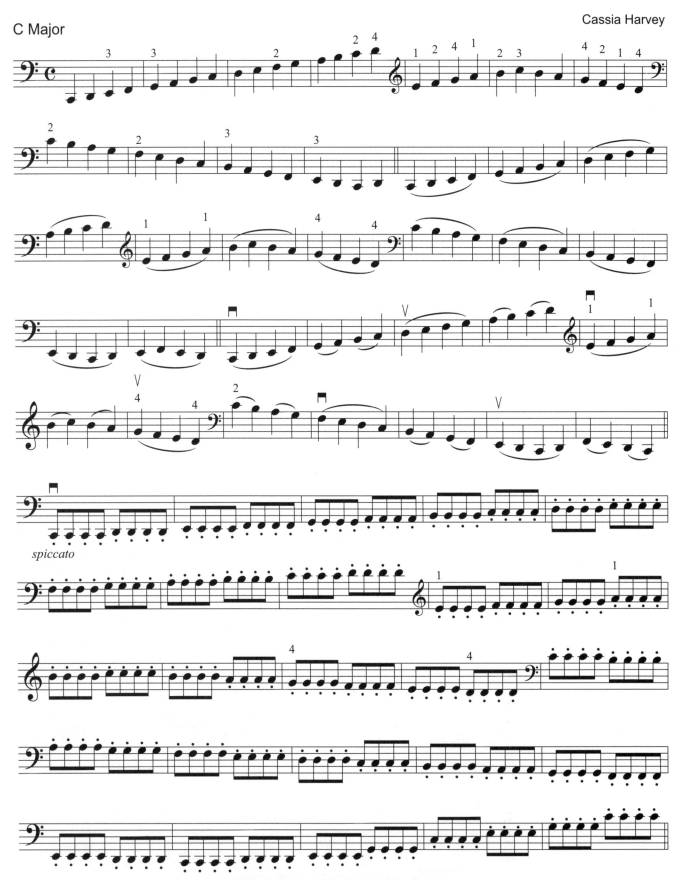

Broken Thirds (One String) for the Cello, Book One
1
Cassia Harvey

Finger Exercises for the Cello, Book Four

First through Seventh Positions   1   Cassia Harvey

Scale Studies (One String) for the Cello, Book One

B♭ major

Cassia Harvey

This entire page is played on the A string.